Amaryllis

"Father," she recognized him for what he was. A reverend, her superior, someone she had insulted in a house of worship. Lumine couldn't help the way longing framed the word as it left her mouth. She had a shameful weakness around authority figures; her craving for guidance, for a parental figure to save her, had always made her attach quickly. Those blue eyes slid back up to her, and she felt warmth coil in her gut that almost made her sick.

Amber Price

Dedication

Dedicated to my frayed patience.

Preface

"Sometimes I touch the things you used to touch, looking for echoes of your fingers."

— Iain Thomas

Acknowledgements

Thank you Kaisa and Grayson for being warm during the writing process of this book. Thank you Genshin Impact for letting me borrow your characters.

CHAPTER ONE

AMARYLLIS

What they were doing was reckless, she thought. His
fingers brushed over hers, radiating warmth that was a
searing contrast to the biting cold that had long claimed
her gloveless hands, igniting a flicker of something
unsettling within her. When she jerked her hand away,
he grasped her wrist, holding it captive as he exhaled hot
air onto her shivering skin. "Thanks," Lumine said
shortly, her voice weak with irritation and gratitude as
she pulled away from him.

Aether eyed her with an intense curiosity, his eyes
matching hers—hues of warm honey framed by lashes
that she knew for a fact didn't mirror hers. She felt the
sharp sting of inadequacy. What was the point of being
identical if she would never be as pretty where it
counted? She breathed out a sigh as he leaned closer to
her. "What's your problem?" His tone was soft and

inquisitive, as though they hadn't had this same conversation more and more over the past few months.

"You know what…" Her voice trailed off, the weight of her words hanging heavy between them. She couldn't bring herself to argue. He'd broken her from being completely confrontational when it came to the subject of their potential adoptions, but he couldn't stop her from feeling bad about it completely. Lumine almost reveled in the resigned huff that escaped him. She was entitled to her own emotions just as much as he was; he couldn't police every feeling she had, as much as she knew he would have liked to.

"I don't want to keep doing it like this," she pressed, her voice trembling with frustration. "We're refusing to be separated, so we're sabotaging each other's adoptions when people try?"

"I know what could happen if someone took you in without me there to protect you," he snapped, his voice tinged with urgency. "They won't let you take your only blood sibling with you—it's suspicious, Lumine." His protectiveness felt suffocating. He snapped at her more and more lately, his greed, and need to have her all to himself rearing their heads under the guise of concern for her. She knew he loathed the thought of being alone as much as she did. But his vehemence outweighed hers. Where she had sadness and resignation, he had a fiery anger that refused to ebb until she agreed over and over again to mess up her own chances at leaving the orphanage.

She shifted on the snow-covered step, lost in her own thoughts, before she was pulled out of them by the slow drag of his fingers over the curve of her cheek. He caressed a part of her hair, the pale blonde that curled delicately around her face. The familiar way he caressed her to comfort her back into submission was working— and she could feel her annoyance leave her as it always did when he treated her so sweetly. Her lids fluttered closed; she could feel her resolve waver before she felt a smile grace her lips. It was more reflex than anything; she knew that he knew that, but it didn't seem to stifle the relief on his face as she gave in. "Okay, okay..." Lumine conceded.

They couldn't be without each other; he refused.

They were putting a new chapel into the orphanage, they said. The reallocation of funding was something the twins weren't sure about anyway. "Aren't sponsors supposed to visit so we can kiss their feet?" Lumine mused aloud, the uncertainty in her tone nothing compared to the way her wide eyes flitted around the beautiful addition to the pitiful infrastructure that was their home.

"Why, Lumi? Is that what you're hungry for breakfast? Shoes?" Aether teased her, leaving her side to walk around. She wondered just where he got the brevity to not be fixed into one spot like she was.

The stained glass cast shimmering reflections across the room, its colors dancing like fleeting hopes, while the winter outside appeared deceptively tranquil compared to how it looked outside her bedroom window when she woke up that morning, the warmth of her twin on her back, his arm secured around her waist. The pews and the pulpit—she was almost afraid to take a step inside; the pristine hardwood floors would get dirty under her cheap secondhand shoes.

Lumine swallowed thickly.

"Now, what are you doing here?" The voice was smooth and chilling, a presence that crept up on her without warning, the heat of breath brushing against her ear. She spun around, her heart racing as she was met with a piercing ice-blue gaze framed by red streaks that seemed to anchor her in place, holding her captive as his arms crossed over his chest, radiating authority. "You two didn't see the warning at the entrance that said they were still making this place presentable? Don't tell me they don't teach the children in here to read." Lumine felt her fingers curl into a fist. Her sudden pique of anger surprised even her; she had become so numb to acting out, letting Aether do it for her for so long that she didn't know what possessed her to open her mouth with a sharp retort ready.

"Don't tell me that you're allowed around children in the first place."

He looked more amused than anything as it left her mouth. He leaned close to her, and she felt her breathing hitch as his arms unfolded, his hand raising to thumb over the bridge of her nose. "You have dirt on you. Try not to look so pathetic," he said simply. Lumine stared at him, the white collar wrapped around his throat, the black uniform that looked like the softest thing she'd ever seen, the cross hanging between them.

"Father," she recognized him for what he was. A reverend, her superior, someone she had insulted in a house of worship. Lumine couldn't help the way longing framed the word as it left her mouth. She had a shameful weakness around authority figures; her craving for guidance, for a parental figure to save her, had always made her attach quickly. Those blue eyes slid back up to her, and she felt warmth coil in her gut that almost made her sick.

"A lamb now, are you?" he mused, his voice low and taunting as he studied her with an intensity that made her skin prickle. His hands came to cradle her cheeks, a gesture both tender and possessive, holding her face captive. "You're quite small for your age—fourteen?" His words dripped with condescension, and she felt her cheeks burn with embarrassment at his incorrect assessment.

"Seventeen."

He clicked his tongue at this.

"Have you even *heard* a sermon before?"

She countered his skepticism with what she wished was some sort of impressive confute, but all she could do was shake her head. Her need for his approval surged as he breathed out a sigh, which she concluded was some show of disappointment and reluctance.

"What's it about?" Lumine asked bravely.

"What is what about? What is a *sermon*?"

Lumine nodded her head, her brows furrowing.

"Figures," he said with a short, sharp laugh. "Let me guess, you think faith is about hope and salvation. Right?" He leaned closer, his voice dropping lower, almost conspiratorial. "Let me teach you something. Faith isn't about you. It's about control. Obedience."

He stepped back just as she made to step closer, his arms crossing again.

"This weekend, come back here." His lips twisted into a knowing smirk, his eyes never leaving hers. "We'll explore a passage together, one that will enlighten you," he said, the corners of his lips curling into a smirk. "I'll break it down for you. The word of the Lord isn't up for interpretation. You listen, you obey." His voice took on an icy edge, and as he leaned in closer, she could feel the weight of his gaze pressing against her. "Otherwise..." His lips curled into a knowing smile, and she felt a chill ripple through her, "you lose your way. And that's when bad things happen."

CHAPTER TWO

LILY

She hadn't shown up on time.

She hadn't expected so many curious teenagers and children to form a sparse crowd around the chapel. They walked past her as she shouldered her way in, their wide eyes lingering on the soft velvets and stain-glass somehow more extravagant than when she'd seen them days ago during the cusp of the chapel's construction. There was a kinship in awe that did nothing to resolve the knot in her chest, but still— Lumine felt an uptick of a smile on her face as she ran her fingers through a smaller girl's hair, appreciating the momentary distraction.

It wasn't like her to venture anywhere by herself. Her hands trembled slightly, hidden beneath the sleeves of her coat, as she willed the adrenaline to fade, the ache that thrummed under her ribs to slow.

"You're here," his voice slid through the thickened air, catching her off guard once again. She hadn't even heard his footsteps, but there he stood, too close, too familiar—like a shadow she could never shake free of. "Albeit late. I suppose it's too much to ask that the children here be able to read or tell time properly. Tsk." his nail ran along the smooth wood of the pew as he approached her, the sound sending a shiver of something up Lumine's spine.

"I'm sorry. My brother didn't want to come."

"And you don't move unless he tells you to, is that right?"

Her lips parted to reply, but the words faltered on her tongue. He was always good at that, it seemed—making her feel like she had a voice, until she didn't. His words sliced through her defenses as if her own thoughts didn't matter, only his. She hated how easily he could silence her, hated how she let him—but something inside her, something she couldn't name, ached to please him. Ached to follow. Like her familial dependence didn't even matter in the grand scheme of her life. And oh how she liked to forget. She tried to focus on the thin billows of smoke that drifted from the snuffed incense on each side of the pulpit.

"I'm here still." there was a note of irritation in her tone, inflating to a scowl and a fold of her arms. anything to conceal the seed of insecurity he had been nurturing since they met.

The reverend leaned in close, scrutinizing her with narrowed eyes. he didn't seem amused this time. didn't seem to have the time for her attitude. She instantly wished she had said something more polite.

"I ordered you to obey and show up and you show me your willingness to learn by stumbling in late. And what are you *wearing*?"

his hand was on her forearm before she could even process the question, the curves of her cheeks shading in embarrassment as he dragged her towards him. he regarded her winter jacket like an abomination, an unsightly thing standing in the way of him sating cold curiosity. Her breath hitched as his fingers grasped the zipper. She should've moved, should've stopped him—but she couldn't. The sound of the zipper was deafening, each slow pull against the metal teeth exposing the thin fabric beneath it. Her pajamas. Humiliation bloomed in her chest, heating her skin, but she stood still. She didn't know why. Maybe it was the way his eyes traced over her, assessing, or the way his voice sounded when he asked questions she couldn't answer. She felt small, like a child caught doing something wrong, but at the same time, there was a part of her that wanted to be seen. There was a sharp intake of breath coming from him as he regarded her appearance.

"I was in a hurry.." Lumine defended lamely.

"Did you *oversleep*?"

She contemplated if lying or the truth would be more acceptable given his blatant annoyance with her. "No." Lumine could feel his eyes on her, he always seemed to have his eyes on her— looking over the expanse of her bare legs, the fabric thin and light blue that clung to her chest and dipped into a V-neck. Cleavage at a church? She felt terribly disrespectful. Her fingers twitched toward the zipper, instinctively trying to shield herself, but his words wrapped around her like a chain, tightening. '*Don't.*' The single command stopped her cold, and she felt the weight of her disobedience in every nerve, her skin prickling beneath his gaze.

She felt his fingers on her chin, tilting up her jaw and canting it this way and that as if she was something to be inspected. despite herself, she became pliant in his hands— her cadence more sulky than anything. She felt his touch move from her jaw and then to her throat, cold fingers slipping around her neck. Lumine squeezed her eyes shut, her face burning. and then—

"Gold suits you." her eyes flutter open, and he's pulling away from her. why is he pulling away? Her hand moved up to the collarbone, fingertips grazing over the cold chill he had left behind on her skin. There was something new there. A chain? No, a necklace? Decorated like some sort of object. The necklace felt heavy, its weight pressing into her skin like a reminder of something she wasn't ready to admit. She didn't want it. She couldn't accept it. But when her fingers traced the gold cross, a small part of her couldn't help but admire how beautiful it looked against her skin. She hated that, too.

"What's this?" she asked quietly, tracing the jewelry down to where it sat prettily over the swell of her breast, an amber pendant tantalizing over pale skin. the citrus of the incense smoke wafted back to her nose and she felt like it was suffocating on it. "I can't accept this." Despite herself, Lumine was infatuated with it. It was too beautiful, too ornate for her.

He laughed humorlessly and she leaned away slightly, angling her body protectively as though he would take it from her. he noticed, how could he not after all? "Do you think you're special?" he cooed, his voice an irritated growl swathed in faux civility. "Look around. Everyone gets one. It's opening day."

Lumine looks around in surprise, her eyes flitting to the necks of multiple orphans to look for glimpses of gold. Similar crucifixes hung so much like hers did. Silvery ornaments of faith, shiny and mirror-like. none of them gold like hers was. when she turned back to him, he was already watching her closely. Why had he given her this, the only one in the entire room that matched the one around his own neck? Her eyes lingered on his chest, she couldn't decide if she felt blessed or trapped.

His blank expression shifts to something more approachable and pleasant when he notices her eyes back on him. "You'll visit the confessional now," he murmured, not bothering to mask the command in his words. The way he said it left no room for refusal, as if her sins were already written on her skin, waiting for him to strip away the layers. His smile didn't reach his eyes as he spoke, the words smooth but laced with an edge that made her heart stutter. "You wouldn't want to leave without cleansing your soul, would you?" The word 'confessional' struck her like a blow, an echo of judgment that made her stomach twist.

He turned his back on her without waiting for a response, already assuming her compliance. And she hated how right he was. Her body moved of its own accord, as if the command had already been etched into her mind, her feet carrying her forward despite the voice in her head screaming to stop. She wasn't sure why. Maybe it was the way his voice had wrapped around her, leaving no room for defiance. Maybe it was the weight of the cross hanging at her chest, like a tether she couldn't break. A part of her screamed to stop, to turn back—but her feet moved anyway, drawn toward him, toward something she didn't understand but couldn't resist. The necklace around her neck like a collar linked by an invisible leash. "Okay."

CHAPTER THREE

ASIATIC

Her fingers traced the loose thread of a worn cotton blanket, tugging as though its unraveling might release the vice coiled around her ribs. The fabric, threadbare and thin, mirrored her own fragile composure—a semblance stretched too tight, fraying at the edges. She had sat through her confession hours ago, yet the weight of scrutiny lingered, an invisible hand pressed mercilessly against her lungs, draining the air from her with each shallow breath.

The confessional booth had been no sanctuary, but a cell —claustrophobic, suffocating, its walls creeping closer with every silent beat. "What is it you seek in confessing to me? Redemption, or validation?" His voice had slithered into her thoughts, a blade wrapped in silk, its edge merciless and unforeseen.

The question struck, lodging in her mind like a barb, leaving her words caught in her throat. "What kind of question is that?" she managed, but her voice betrayed her—a tremor of uncertainty lacing each syllable.

"The critical thinking kind," he purred, his tone a curious blend of mockery and a sickly sweetness that seemed to coat the air between them. "Let's test if your mind is capable of something so trivial." She flinched, warmth blooming in her cheeks as shame twisted inside her. Had she truly been so naive? Her fingers curled, nails digging into her palms as she fought to hold herself steady, to conjure an answer that would not render her **pathetic**.

"Redemption."

"Is that right?" There was a lilt in his tenor, an almost breathy uptick of satisfaction that made her pause. But Lumine wasn't sure if she'd answered correctly. The confessional felt suffocating again, the walls pressing in closer as silence stretched between them. "Redemption," he repeated, rolling the word around his mouth like it was a bitter taste. "You say it so easily. But have you even earned it? No. You want to be forgiven without doing the work. You want to be cleansed without ever getting your hands dirty. That's not redemption—that's cowardice *at best.*"

He did not wait for elaboration; his gaze pierced through her silence, his presence unyielding as he transitioned to the next probing question in his relentless assessment.

"When you look in the mirror, do you see someone worthy of salvation, or someone who deserves to suffer?" The question reverberated through her mind, his voice lingering like a shadow long after it had faded.

She faltered, her fingers curling tighter around the thin fabric as though it could shield her from the answer lurking beneath layers of shame and doubt. The response she wished to give remained elusive, buried under guilt that weighed heavy, refusing to yield.

Her gaze flitted toward the dim silhouette behind the screen, seeking some trace of empathy or malice. But he remained still, a figure carved from shadow, waiting—unyielding, patient, a figure eager to watch her unravel.

"Do you intend to suffer, or not? Do you see a victim? A liar?" he pressed, voice sharp with impatience. "Isn't that why you're here—begging for scraps of salvation you'll never receive?"

"No." The word escaped her too quickly, a reflex she

regretted the moment it left her lips. It felt sour on her tongue, hollow, as though spoken by someone else. And a treacherous thought nagged at her—what if it wasn't true?

"What is your relationship with your sibling?"

The question sliced through her, unexpected. Her breath stilled, fingers digging into the blanket as her heart thudded painfully against her ribcage. She hadn't prepared herself for this, for him to drag Aether into her confessions, into this exposed, raw moment.

"I... my brother. His name is Aether." Her voice was barely a whisper, as if she could hide him in the softness of her admission, hoping the priest wouldn't press further, wouldn't detect the tremor woven into each syllable. But she knew better than to expect mercy.

He made a low, dismissive hum—a sound that coiled in her stomach, tightening with each second. It was acknowledgment, but hollow, as though her confession was merely an amusement, something to be picked apart. "Another insignificant lamb," he murmured, and his laugh, low and pitiless, made her skin prickle. "I'm sure his righteousness keeps you warm at night. How quaint." He paused, a cruel smirk curling through his

words. "But you don't need him, do you? You're stronger
without him pulling your strings."

"He's not—" The denial fell from her lips instinctively,
yet even as she said it, doubt crept in, a flicker of
uncertainty that caught in her throat.

"So, you and your brother—inseparable, I imagine?" His
words dripped with venomous sarcasm, each syllable a
smirk laced with malice. "Or is he just another chain
wrapped around that slender neck of yours?" His
disinterest was palpable, as though her response
mattered only to his amusement, yet the question
lingered in the air, pressing down on her like an unseen
weight.

"No," she admitted finally, her voice a soft exhale of
defeat. "No, we don't... we don't get along well."

Her confessor released a soft, derisive sound—
somewhere between a hum and a scowl. "Why not?" he
inquired, his tone slick with feigned curiosity, like a
predator toying with its prey. "What is it about him that
grates at you so much? His face? His presence? His
weakness?"

"No," she responded sharply, her voice rising,

instinctively defensive. "It's not that. It's..." She faltered, words eluding her, tangled in the web of emotions she had long kept buried.

She struggled to silence the taunting lilt in his voice, desperate to unearth some semblance of clarity from her own thoughts. For the first time, she was confronting a truth she had never dared to admit aloud—that she and Aether might not be as united as she had wanted to believe. She hadn't come here for guidance, but there it was, tempting her, stirring something restless and painful in her chest.

She shouldn't say it. She shouldn't admit it.

"He won't let me be adopted." The confession fell from her lips, a delicate fracture in her armor, the last word breaking as if split by the weight it carried. And as the silence settled, she felt something lift from within—a burden finally released, yet leaving her trembling, exposed, and raw.

"Ah, now we're getting somewhere," he murmured, a twisted smirk shaping each word. "He won't let you be adopted? Clinging to you like a parasite, isn't he? Tell me—how does it feel, knowing you're bound to someone you'll never be able to abandon... yet who will never set you free?"

Lumine bit her lip, memories stirring like dust in an abandoned room. She saw them as children—small, inseparable, playing with the others in the yard, scouring the ground for bugs, sneaking into the kitchen at midnight to share food, laughing over a birthday cake meant for a staff member. But as they grew older, something shifted. Aether's refusal to let go clashed with her own desperate urge to latch onto anyone or anything that might finally rescue her.

She remembered the first time he'd sabotaged her adoption. She'd been fourteen—wide-eyed, hopeful, thrilled that she had been chosen. She couldn't recall the faces of that family anymore, only the feeling of belonging she'd tasted for a moment. They had a small child, a little one she could protect, be the older sibling for once, a role she had always yearned for. But the family had only wanted her.

Not both of them.

She could still feel the weight of Aether clinging to her neck that night, his arms wrapped around her so tightly it hurt. Lumine's hands had moved reflexively, stroking his back as her mind stumbled to process the future she'd lost—a new family, a new life—all slipping through her fingers. Gone, as quickly as it had appeared. She didn't know what to feel.

But Aether was sobbing, a rarity, his face buried in her shoulder. Aether, who never cried, who always held things together. He needed her then, didn't he? So she'd let him cling, let him apologize over and over, his whispered excuses, his lips brushing against her neck as he held her captive in his trembling embrace.

When his apologies quieted and his breaths turned ragged, he'd lifted his head to meet her gaze. His eyes were red and swollen, a blend of shame and something darker that made her stomach tighten. *"You forgive me, right?"* His voice held a new steadiness, but his clenched fists betrayed his tangible unease.

Lumine's lips parted to answer, but Aether moved before she could utter a sound. His mouth crashed against hers, silencing any semblance of words. Her body froze, paralyzed as a cold shock spread through her limbs. His lips trembled against hers, hot and frantic, and for a fleeting, unbearable moment, Lumine didn't know how to react.

When he pulled back, his expression was a twisted

reflection of her own—a mingling of shock, guilt, and raw panic. He shoved her back, almost violently, as though he couldn't bear to be near her, and stumbled away, leaving her standing there, trembling and numb, with the bitter taste of his kiss still lingering.

They never spoke of it.

"Sometimes... I get nervous," Lumine admitted, the once suffocating walls of the confessional losing their novelty, now it was just a room. a room that was a safe for her guilt-ridden secrets.

Scaramouche let the silence settle, savoring her admission like a hunter savoring his prey's surrender. Finally, he spoke, his tone laced with a dark satisfaction. "You get nervous? Around him?"

Her heart thundered in her chest, each beat a dull thud that echoed louder than her whispered confession. She nodded, but then realized he couldn't see her through the screen. "Yes," she breathed, the word barely more than a murmur, yet it felt like baring herself raw.

"You're afraid of him." It was not a question but a statement, one that twisted like a knife in her stomach. "He begged you for forgiveness, didn't he?"

Scaramouche's voice softened mockingly, mimicking Aether's desperation. "Did you enjoy it? Watching him grovel, hoping you'd absolve him? Or did it make you sick, knowing he'd never let you go?" His tone sharpened, a blade carving into her restraint. "What did you say when he kissed you? Did you say anything at all?"

"No. No, I—" Her voice faltered, the denial weak even as it left her lips. Was she afraid of Aether? The brother who had been both her protector and captor, the one who never left her side. But that memory... that kiss...

It gnawed at her, an intrusive thought she could neither shake nor reconcile. Aether hadn't meant it, she assured herself, clinging to the excuse. He'd been desperate, lost. But the weight of that moment lingered, festering in the silence they'd kept between them ever since.

"Then why the nerves?" Scaramouche's voice dripped with false gentleness, drawing her deeper, binding her in a web of her own admission.

Lumine closed her eyes, fingers digging into the booth's leather. "It's not fear. It's... guilt." The word tasted acrid, like ash in her mouth- it stuck to her teeth and lingered long after she said it, but it was the closest thing to truth she could find. "I feel like I'm abandoning him. He's always needed me. But I can't... I can't keep doing this."

"Doing what?" he pressed.

"Sacrificing myself. For him." The words escaped, fractured and raw, like shards of glass she'd kept buried for years. "He sabotages every chance I have. And I let him."

"Is that the lie you tell yourself? That you can be saved?" His chuckle was low, mocking. "How tragically naive. You're drowning in sins you don't even dare to name. Yet here you are, pretending you can still surface, still breathe." There was a pause, and she felt the weight of his gaze through the screen, sharp and penetrating. Then he spoke again, his voice thick with satisfaction. "So, you finally admit it. He's the chain around your neck. And you're too weak to sever it. How sweet. It must be a comfort, knowing he'd rather see you both rot together than let you find 'happiness' without him."

The accusation cut deep, but she didn't flinch, didn't attempt to deny it. The truth was suffocating, bitter and unyielding, but she let it settle around her, no longer resisting.

"...Yes," she breathed, the word almost threatening, conspiratory. "He is."

www.ingramcontent.com/pod-product-compliance
Lightning Source LLC
LaVergne TN
LVHW021329200726

843509LV00014B/2451